PRESENTED BY

Kate Welch

Reading

in honor of

Princeton University

SMYTHE GAMBRELL
LIBRARY

WESTMINSTER
SCHOOLS

Derek Warnick
1993

HENRY MOORE

From Bones and Stones to Sketches and Sculptures

JANE MYLUM GARDNER

FOUR WINDS PRESS ✳ New York

MAXWELL MACMILLAN CANADA   Toronto   MAXWELL MACMILLAN INTERNATIONAL   New York   Oxford   Singapore   Sydney

ACKNOWLEDGMENTS

The journey this project has made from idea to book has been successfully completed because of the help of some very talented and compassionate people. First, I would like to thank the Henry Moore Foundation and especially Angela Dyer, Publications Editor. Mrs. Dyer participated throughout every phase of the project and was always willing to give her prompt and expert advice. I would also like to thank Mrs. Dyer's assistant, Janet Iliffe, for the special care she took in coordinating the photographs in this book.

I am grateful, too, for the additional photographs provided by Professor John Hedgecoe of the Royal College of Art in London, Gemma Levine, and Bill Ross of the University of New Hampshire. I have not found a way to thank David Finn, who was kind enough to walk that extra mile with me. Mr. Finn generously contributed by making photographs for the book's front and back covers.

Katherine Kirkpatrick, my editor at Four Winds Press, Art Director Christy Hale, and Editor in Chief Virginia Duncan proved to be a world-class team to work with. Last, but not least, there were friends who made all the difference. Though the list is too long to name everyone, I must acknowledge Dani Adjemovitch, Caroline Goldsmith, Ella Annelli, William Kaye, and Christine Matthews for helping to make the journey possible.

To my parents, Jack and Rebecca Mylum

A work of art is the expression of the spirit.
—HENRY MOORE

Each morning Henry Moore bicycled through the garden on the way to work in his studio.

Henry Moore was a sculptor. He was a hardworking Englishman from Yorkshire. When he wasn't sculpting, Henry was drawing. With just a break for lunch, he worked from early in the morning until late in the afternoon.

Scattered about the studio where he worked were natural shapes Henry found while walking in the fields near his house. When an unusual object caught his eye, Henry picked it up and brought it back to the studio for a closer, longer look.

Animal bones, a bird's skeleton, weathered pieces of wood, and a handful of shells, pebbles, and flint had found their way onto the shelves in his studio. Over the years the collection had grown. It even included an old elephant's skull someone had given him.

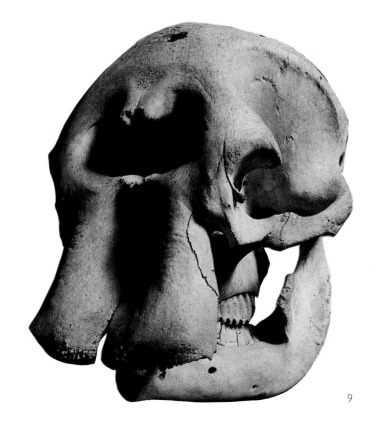

The bones and stones, pebbles and shells gave Henry ideas. The shapes slept in his mind. They sparked Henry's imagination and blended with other ideas. Days later as he was drawing the shapes from memory, Henry's thoughts became sketches.

If Henry liked one of the drawings from his sketchbook, he made a small model of it in plaster. These little models, called maquettes, were small enough for him to hold in the palm of his hand.

One look at a maquette was never enough for Henry. Before he decided whether he liked the maquette, he looked at it again and again.

His eyes and fingers followed the curves over and around.

He looked at each side of the maquette.

He even looked at it upside down. Henry looked slowly.   Henry sometimes carved

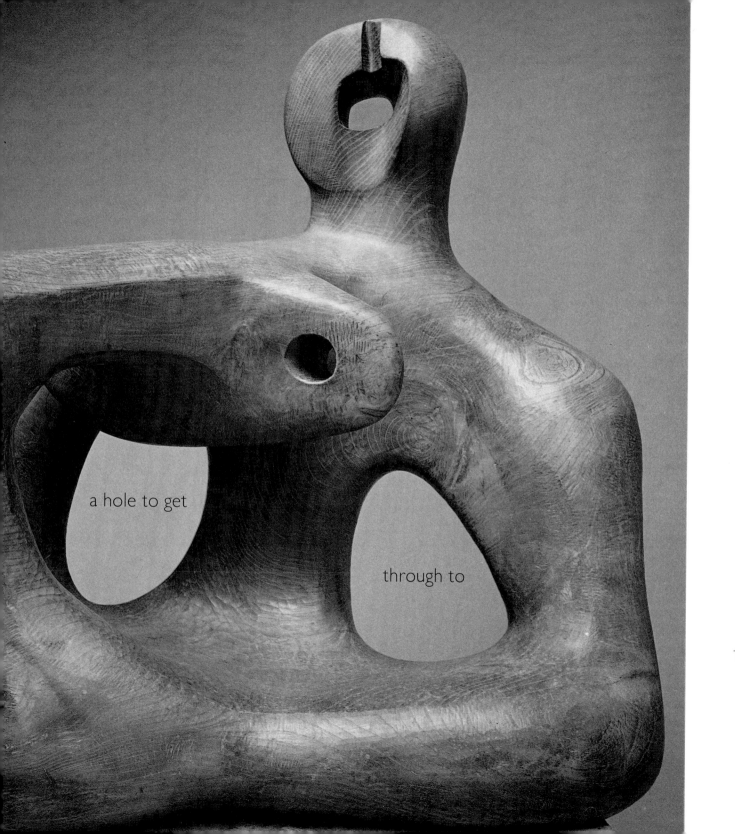

a hole to get

through to

the other side.

The bones and stones, pebbles and shells inspired ideas for Henry's sketches and sculptures.

One shape led to another. When Henry worked on a plaster maquette, a layer of white dust covered the studio.

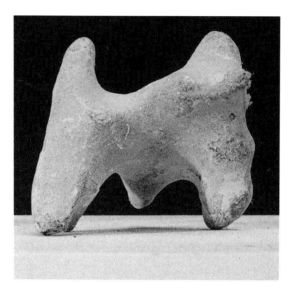

If Henry still thought a maquette was interesting after a few months, then he'd often make an even larger model. If he liked the larger model, he would make a bigger one still. The material he usually chose for his large sculptures was bronze.

Henry carved some sculptures in stone, and some he carved in wood.

Day after day Henry carefully chipped away the shapes. He worked his way around a sculpture, until at last the chipping away stopped. When the shapes felt and looked just right, the sculpture was finished, and then Henry gave it a name.

Next to the studio where Henry worked, sheep grazed in the pasture. Across the pasture stood the Sheep Piece, a bronze sculpture Henry had made. The lambs and sheep played around the sculpture.

Often Henry glanced at the sheep through the window in his studio. The sheep had all looked alike to Henry until the day he began sketching them. Then he saw how different one sheep was from another.

Most often the shapes that Henry sketched and sculpted were female figures.
Over the years Henry carved many different mother and child sculptures.

Flints from the fields inspired some of the mother and child shapes. When his daughter, Mary, was four, Henry made a toy for her, which he named the Rocking Chair.

Families were a subject so important, so captivating to Henry that he drew them over and over again. Henry's feelings about his own family inspired the silent shapes that he drew and carved.

Henry spent many years working on his sculptures while his wife, Irina, was hard at work in her garden. Every day Henry rode his bicycle down the path toward the house, past the apple trees, past his sculptures in Irina's beautiful garden. They stopped working long enough to eat lunch together, usually a plate of cold meat and pickles, Henry's favorite.

Henry preferred to look at his sculptures out-of-doors. He enjoyed seeing the sculptures warmed by the light of a clear sky or cooled by the dim mist of a gray, rainy day. Henry liked seeing his sculptures as the colors in the garden changed from one season to the next.

In gardens around the world his sculptures sit waiting to be discovered and touched. Henry once remarked, *"If at first you don't understand what you see, then look again or make a sketch. Give your imagination a chance to grow!*

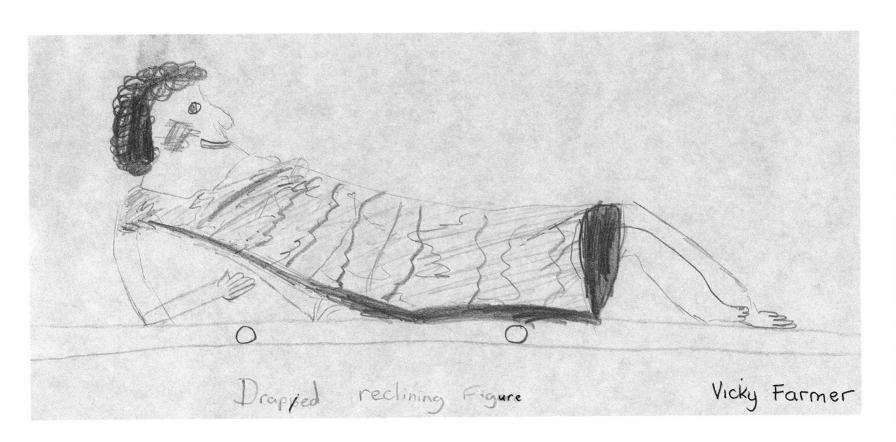

Drapped reclining Figure   Vicky Farmer

"Art has everything to do with life. A work of art is the expression of the spirit.... This is what matters more than a beautiful or perfect work of art."

A BIOGRAPHICAL NOTE ABOUT HENRY MOORE

Henry Spencer Moore was born in 1898 in Castleford, England, in the region known as Yorkshire. He was the seventh of eight children born to Raymond and Mary Baker Moore. Raymond Moore worked in the coal mines to support the family. He was a strict father and had high ambitions for his children. Henry was brought up to believe that everything is possible for those who work hard.

At the age of ten, Henry told his father he wanted to be a sculptor when he grew up. Raymond Moore's advice to his young son was, "Lad, you have to learn how to put food on the table first. Then, you can become an artist if that's what you want."

After he fought in World War I, Henry entered Leeds School of Art on a government scholarship. Because of his own hard work and talent, Henry was offered a chance to further his studies at the Royal College of Art in London. In 1925 at the age of twenty-seven, Henry finished his graduate studies and started his career as a sculptor.

After Henry's short courtship with Irina Radetzky, a beautiful young Russian painter, the two wed on July 27, 1929. As an Official War Artist during World War II, Henry drew many pictures of people sheltering at night in the underground railway stations. His drawings inspired so many of his fellow countrymen that before the war was over, Henry's work was known and admired throughout Britain. In 1946 Henry and Irina's only child, a daughter named Mary, was born.

Henry was fond of children, and it was said that he often enjoyed conversations with children more than those with adults. He was never too busy to spend time answering children's questions whenever they visited his studio or Irina's garden at their home, Hoglands, in Much Hadham, England, the setting for most of the pictures in this book. The drawings of Henry's sculptures were done by schoolchildren from Barnsley, England, who sketched Henry's work during their visit to the Yorkshire Sculpture Park.

Henry felt strongly that his sculpture was an art of the open air, and that the best possible background for his work was the sky. Many of his large sculptures can be seen out-of-doors or in gardens and public places all over the world. Some of Henry's work is not so easily understood at first glance. Often, walking around the sculpture, touching it, and allowing time for thoughtful looking or sketching of the shapes will help the viewer enjoy what may first be overlooked.

Henry Moore worked as a sculptor for sixty years, and during his long career he produced an exceptionally large quantity of work. His favorite themes were forms he considered to be of enduring importance: the reclining female figure, the family group, the mother and child. Often his ideas blended the human figure with shapes and textures from nature. In sculptures that range from the intimate to the monumental in size, Henry Moore's work elevated the human figure, giving it a sense of dignity and expressing Henry's deepest feelings about life. He

abandoned the ideal of a perfect model of beauty and focused instead on capturing the essence, or spirit, of the subjects he carved. When Henry died in 1986, many people said that he had become the most famous British sculptor of all time, while others said he was the most famous sculptor of the twentieth century.

PHOTOGRAPHIC ACKNOWLEDGMENTS

The publisher would like to thank the following for permission to reproduce photographs:

David Finn: front and back covers, pages 20, 32
John Hedgecoe: pages 5, 8, 27
Gemma Levine: pages 12, 18
Widlund, Courtesy of University of New Hampshire: page 23 (right)

All photographs except the above were supplied by and reproduced by permission of the Henry Moore Foundation. Many of the photographs of the sculptures were taken by Henry Moore.

LH numbers of sculptures refer to the catalogue numbers in *Henry Moore: Complete Sculpture*, published by Lund Humphries, London, 1944–88; *HMF* numbers of drawings refer to the Henry Moore Foundation archive of drawings.

Front and back covers and page 32: **Reclining Figure.** 1969. Bronze, 11'3" long (LH608).

Inside flaps: **Large Totem Head.** 1968. Bronze, 8'2" high (LH 577).

Title page (right): **Mother and Child.** 1932. Carved concrete, 7" high (LH 120).

Page 3: **Rocking Chair No. 1.** 1950. Bronze, 12½" high (LH 274).

Page 10 (below): **Page from Sketchbook B: Reclining Figure (from Bone).** 1935. Black chalk and pencil, 5½" × 8¾" (HMF 1210v).

Page 11: **Page from Sketchbook: Sculpture Ideas in Settings and Drawing for Detroit Reclining Figure.** 1938. Pencil, 7⅜" × 10⅞" (HMF 1416).

Pages 14, 15: **Reclining Figure.** 1939. Elmwood, 6'9" long (LH 210).

Page 17: **Three Way Piece No. 2: Archer.** 1964–65. Bronze, 10'8" high (LH 535).

Page 19: **Reclining Figure: Holes.** 1976–78. 7'3" long (LH 657).

Page 20: **Sheep Piece.** 1971–72. Bronze, 18' high (LH 627).

Page 21 (above): **Page 23 from Sheep Sketchbook: Fat Lambs.** 1972. Wash and ballpoint pen, 8¼" × 9⅞" (HMF 3339).

Page 21 (below): **Page 45 from Sheep Sketchbook: Head.** 1972. Ballpoint pen, 8¼" × 9⅞" (HMF 3361).

Page 22 (left): **Mother and Child.** 1949. Bronze, 2'8" high (LH 269b).

Page 22 (right): **Mother and Child.** 1931. Sycamore wood, 30" high (LH 106).

Page 23 (center): **Rocking Chair No. 1.** 1950. Bronze, 12½" high (LH 274).

Page 24 (left): **Family Groups.** 1944. Chalk, pen, and watercolor, 19½" × 12½" (HMF 2230).

Page 24 (right): Detail from **Two Studies for a Family Group.** 1944. Crayon and watercolor, 21¾" × 12⅝" (HMF 2228).

Page 25: **Family Group.** 1948–49. Bronze, 5' high (LH 269).

Page 28: **Draped Reclining Figure.** 1952–53. Bronze, 5'2" long (LH 336).

Page 29: Drawing by Vicky Farmer
Page 31: Drawing by Robert James Lees